Contents

Cheese Frosting 3

Ritz Stew 3

Cinnamon Pumpkin Loaves 4

Crunchy Amish Coleslaw With Nutmeg Dressing 6

Friendship Pancakes 8

Creamy Potato And Bread Casserole 9

Juniper Stir Fry 10

Hot Cornmeal 11

Slow Burger Stew 12

Traditional Peanut Butter 13

Sugar Pie 14

Fried Tunnel Cakes 15

Green Stew Pan 17

Creamy Jell-O And Egg Salad 18

Chicken Farm Soup 19

Creamy Chicken Roast 20

Applesauce Muffins 21

Vanilla Coffee Cake 23

Banana Cake With Vanilla Frosting 24

Vanilla Blondies 26

Amish Mint Tea 27

Crunchy Broccoli With Cheddar Sauce 29

Condensed Maple Tart 30

Salisbury Steak With Mushroom Sauce 31

Quick Corn And Egg Soup 33

Sweet Spicy Raisins Sauce 34

Rhubarb Rolls With Vanilla Sauce 35

Caramen Pecan Cake 37

Starte Amish Biscuits 39

Endive Salad With Bacon Dressing 41

Homemade Ketchup 42

Classic Cheese Corn 43

Peanut Crackers 44

Sweet And Salty Beef Chili 45

Sunnycornbread 47

Glazed Crisco Puffs 48

Valentine Strawberry Amish Bread 50

Spicy Orange Bread 51

Poppy Bread 53

Splenda Muffins 54

Nutty Carrot Muffins 56

CHEESE FROSTING

Prep Time:5 mins- **Total Time:** 5 mins

SERVINGS : 1

NUTRITIONAL VALUE

Calories 1826.2 , Fat 115.7g , Cholesterol 249.9mg , Sodium 1099.1mg , Carbohydrates 188.9g , Protein 15.5g

INGREDIENTS

- 8 oz. cream cheese
- 1/8 tsp salt
- 2/3 C. brown sugar
- 2 C. Cool Whip
- 1 tsp vanilla

DIRECTIONS

Step 1

Get a large mixing bowl: Cream in it the cream cheese, sugar, vanilla and salt until they become light and smooth.

Step 2

Stir in the cool whip. Place the frosting in the fridge until ready to use.

Step 3

Enjoy.

RITZ STEW

Prep Time: 5 mins- **Total Time:** 15 mins

SERVINGS : 4

NUTRITIONAL VALUE

Calories 268.4 , Fat 16.8g , Cholesterol 32.3mg , Sodium 360.5mg , Carbohydrates 23.6g , Protein 6.1g

INGREDIENTS

- 2 tbsp butter

- 2 C. milk

- 1 (4 oz.) packet Ritz

DIRECTIONS

Step 1

Place a heavy saucepan over medium heat. Stir in the butter until it melts and become slightly brown.

Step 2

Stir in the milk and heat it through.

Step 3

Get a large mixing bowl: Place in it the crackers. Pour the milk mix all over them and let sit for a while.

Step 4

Serve your ritz for breakfast.

Step 5

Enjoy.

CINNAMON PUMPKIN LOAVES

Prep Time: 15 mins- **Total Time:** 1 hr 15 mins

SERVINGS : 1

NUTRITIONAL VALUE

Calories 3140.3 , Fat 121.9g , Cholesterol 423.0mg , Sodium 3734.8mg , Carbohydrates 484.9g , Protein 37.6g

INGREDIENTS

- 3 C. sugar

- 1 tsp cinnamon

- 1 C. vegetable oil

- 1 tsp allspice

- 4 eggs, beaten

- 1 tsp nutmeg

- 1 (1 lb) can pumpkin

- 2/3 C. water

- 3 1/2 C. flour

- 1 C. chopped nuts

- 2 tsp baking soda

- 2 tsp salt

- 1/2 tsp clove

DIRECTIONS

Step 1

Before you do anything, preheat the oven to 350 F. Grease 4 bread pans and place them aside.

Step 2

Get a large mixing bowl: Beat in it the sugar, oil and eggs.

Step 3

Mix in the pumpkin followed by the flour, baking soda salt, clove, cinnamon, allspice, nutmeg and water at last.

Step 4

Fold the nuts into the batter and pour it into the pans. Place them in the oven and let them cook for 60 min.

Step 5

Allow bread loaves to cool down completely then serve them.

Step 6

Enjoy.

CRUNCHY AMISH COLESLAW WITH NUTMEG DRESSING

Prep Time: 10 mins- **Total Time:** 15 mins

SERVINGS : 5

NUTRITIONAL VALUE

Calories 160.0 , Fat 7.7g , Cholesterol 100.7mg , Sodium 664.6mg , Carbohydrates 19.0g , Protein 5.0g

INGREDIENTS

- DRESSING

- 1 large shredded carrot

- 2 large eggs

- 1 celery, chopped

- 3 tbsp granulated sugar

- 1 small onion, chopped

- 1 1/2 tbsp all-purpose flour

- 1/2 green bell pepper, chopped

- 1 1/4 tsp salt

- 1/4 C. minced parsley

- 1/2 tsp ground mustard

- 1 1/2 tsp celery seeds

- 1/4 C. cider vinegar

- 1 tsp mustard seeds

- 1/4 C. water

- 1/2 tsp coarse ground black pepper

- 1 tbsp butter

- 3 tbsp cream

- COLESLAW

- 6 C. shredded cabbage

DIRECTIONS

Step 1

Get a heavy saucepan. Whisk in it the eggs then add to them the sugar, flour, salt and mustard gradually while mixing all the time.

Step 2

Mix in the vinegar and the water followed by oil and butter until you get a smooth mix.

Step 3

Let the dressing cook over low heat for 7 min while stirring it all the time until they become creamy.

Step 4

Add to them the cream and whisk them well. Place it aside to cool down completely.

Step 5

Get a large mixing bowl: Stir in it all the veggies with mustard seeds, salt and pepper.

Step 6

Drizzle the dressing over them and toss them to coat. Place the salad in the fridge until ready to serve.

Step 7

Enjoy.

FRIENDSHIP PANCAKES

Prep Time: 5 mins- **Total Time:** 25 mins

SERVINGS : 4

NUTRITIONAL VALUE

Calories 215.1 , Fat 9.4g , Cholesterol 50.7mg , Sodium 169.5mg , Carbohydrates 25.9g , Protein 5.8g

INGREDIENTS

- 1 egg

- 1 1/2 tsp baking powder

- 1 C. Amish starter

- 1 C. flour

- 1/2 C. milk

- 2 tbsp oil

- 1 tsp vanilla

DIRECTIONS

Step 1

Get a large mixing bowl: Cream in it the egg with Amish starter, milk, oil and vanilla.

Step 2

Beat in it the flour with baking powder. Mix in a splash of milk if the batter is too thick.

Step 3

Place a griddle over medium heat. Grease it with a cooking spray. Spread in it 1/4 C. of the pancake batter.

Step 4

Let it cook until it becomes golden brown on each side. Repeat the process with the remaining batter.

Step 5

Serve your pancakes with your favorite toppings.

Step 6

Enjoy.

Step 7

CREAMY POTATO AND BREAD CASSEROLE

Prep Time: 10 mins- **Total Time:** 50 mins

SERVINGS : 6

NUTRITIONAL VALUE

Calories 213.1 , Fat 11.7g , Cholesterol 6.9mg , Sodium 150.1mg , Carbohydrates 23.6g , Protein 5.0g

INGREDIENTS

- 1 1/2 C. turnips, grated

- 2 medium onions, chopped

- 1 1/2 C. potatoes, grated

- 1 tbsp dried parsley

- 3/4 C. milk

- 1/2 tsp pepper

- 1/2 C. plain yogurt

- salt

- 1/2 C. whole wheat bread crumbs

- 1/4 C. vegetable oil

DIRECTIONS

Step 1

Before you do anything, preheat the oven to 375 F. Grease casserole dish and place it aside.

Step 2

Get a large mixing bowl: Combine in it the turnips with potato, milk, yogurt, oil, onion, parsley, pepper and salt.

Step 3

Pour the mix into the casserole dish. Top it with the breadcrumbs. Place the casserole in the oven and let it cook for 42 min. Serve it hot.

Step 4

Enjoy.

JUNIPER STIR FRY

Prep Time: 10 mins- **Total Time:** 1 hr 20 mins

SERVINGS : 6

NUTRITIONAL VALUE

Calories 130.8 , Fat 10.3g , Cholesterol 1.2mg , Sodium 558.4mg , Carbohydrates 8.2g , Protein 2.4g

INGREDIENTS

- 1/4 C. walnut oil

- 7 -8 juniper berries

- 1 tbsp white mustard seeds

- 1 1/2 tbsp red bell peppers, chopped

- 1 medium onion, sliced

- 1 C. chicken stock

- 1 lb sauerkraut, drained

- 1 1/2 tbsp ginger, minced

DIRECTIONS

Step 1

Place a heavy saucepan over medium heat. Heat the oil in it. Stir in the mustard seeds and cook them for 40 sec.

Step 2

Mix in the onion and let it cook for 12 min over low heat with the lid on. Mix in the stock, sauerkraut, ginger, and juniper berries.

Step 3

Put on the lid and let them cook for 60 min. Serve your stir fry with bell pepper.

Step 4

Enjoy.

HOT CORNMEAL

Prep Time: 5 mins- **Total Time:** 25 mins

SERVINGS : 8

NUTRITIONAL VALUE

Calories 55.2 , Fat 0.5g , Cholesterol 0.0mg , Sodium 298.6mg , Carbohydrates 11.7g , Protein 1.2g

INGREDIENTS

- 3 C. water

- 1 tsp salt

- 1 C. cornmeal

DIRECTIONS

Step 1

Grease a baking pan and place it aside.

Step 2

Place a large saucepan over medium heat. Stir in the water with cornmeal and salt. Put on the lid and let it cook for 15 to 20 min or until it is done.

Step 3

Pour the mixture into the greased pan. Place it aside let it sit unit it lose heat completely. Slice it into squares.

Step 4

Place a large pan over medium heat. Heat in it a splash of oil. Cook in it the corn squares until they become golden brown then serve them.

Step 5

Enjoy.

SLOW BURGER STEW

Prep Time: 10 mins- **Total Time:** 8 hrs 10 mins

SERVINGS : 4

NUTRITIONAL VALUE

Calories 102.0 , Fat 0.4g , Cholesterol 0.0mg , Sodium 1381.1mg , Carbohydrates 23.0g , Protein 3.3g

INGREDIENTS

- 2 C. hamburger

- 1 C. diced green pepper

- 2 C. sliced raw potatoes

- 2 C. canned tomatoes

- 2 C. chopped celery

- 1/2 C. diced onion

- 2 tsp salt

- 1/4 tsp pepper

DIRECTIONS

Step 1

Combine all the ingredients in a slow cooker. Put on the lid and let them cook for 7 h on low. Serve it hot.

Step 2

Enjoy.

TRADITIONAL PEANUT BUTTER

Prep Time: 10 mins- **Total Time:** 10 mins

SERVINGS : 1

NUTRITIONAL VALUE

Calories 1270.7 , Fat 43.9g , Cholesterol 0.0mg , Sodium 565.9mg , Carbohydrates 221.2g , Protein 21.8g

INGREDIENTS

- 1/2 C. creamy peanut butter

- 1 C. light corn syrup

- 1/4 C. marshmallow crème

DIRECTIONS

Step 1

Get a large mixing bowl: Combine in it all the ingredients and beat them until they become smooth.

Step 2

Transfer the mix to a container and place it in the fridge until ready to serve.

Step 3

Enjoy.

SUGAR PIE

Prep Time: 15 mins- **Total Time:** 1 hr 15 mins

SERVINGS : 4

NUTRITIONAL VALUE

Calories 2656.2 , Fat 115.4g , Cholesterol 622.0mg , Sodium 1379.8mg , Carbohydrates 387.8g , Protein 28.9g

INGREDIENTS

- 1/3 C. butter

- 1/2 C. evaporated milk

- 1 1/2 C. brown sugar

- 1 9" unbaked pie shell

- 2 eggs

- 1 tbsp all-purpose flour

DIRECTIONS

Step 1

Before you do anything, preheat the oven to 350 F. Grease a pie pan and place it aside.

Step 2

Get a large mixing bowl: Cream in it the butter, brown sugar, eggs, flour, and milk.

Step 3

Place the shell in the pan and pour the filling into it. Place it in the oven and let it cook for 16 min.

Step 4

Allow it to cool down completely for 1 h in the oven then serve it with your favorite toppings.

Step 5

Enjoy.

FRIED TUNNEL CAKES

Prep Time: 10 mins- **Total Time:** 15 mins

SERVINGS : 6

NUTRITIONAL VALUE

Calories 349.3 , Fat 6.0g , Cholesterol 117,1mg , Sodium 390.9mg , Carbohydrates 60.3g , Protein 12.2g

INGREDIENTS

- 3 -4 C. flour
- 1/2 tsp salt
- 3 eggs
- powdered sugar
- 2 C. milk

- oil

- 1/4 C. sugar

- 2 tsp baking powder

DIRECTIONS

Step 1

Before you do anything, preheat the oven to 350 F.

Step 2

Get a large mixing bowl: Cream in it the egg with milk and sugar.

Step 3

Get a mixing bowl: Stir in it the flour with baking powder and salt. Add it to the eggs mix and combine them well.

Step 4

Pour 1 C. of the butter in a funnel with an half inch opening.

Step 5

Place a heavy pan over medium heat and heat in it about 1/8 inch of oil.

Step 6

Squeeze the funnel to get the batter out into the hot oil drizzling it in circular and messy motion until you get a 6 to 8 inches cake.

Step 7

Cook the cake in the hot oil until it become golden brown on each side.

Step 8

Repeat the process with the remaining ingredients. Serve your golden cakes with your favorite toppings.

Step 9

Enjoy.

GREEN STEW PAN

Prep Time: 20 mins- **Total Time:** 50 mins

SERVINGS : 6

NUTRITIONAL VALUE

Calories 173.4 , Fat 10.4g , Cholesterol 15.4mg , Sodium 771.7mg , Carbohydrates 16.7g , Protein 5.2g

INGREDIENTS

- 6 slices turkey bacon
- 1/2 tsp pepper
- 3 medium onions, sliced
- 1/3 C. boiling water
- 1 lb fresh green beans, cleaned and cut
- into small pieces
- 2 C. fresh diced tomatoes
- 1 tsp salt

DIRECTIONS

Step 1

Place a large pan over medium heat. Cook in it the bacon until it become crisp.

Step 2

Stir in the onion and let it cook for 10 min while stirring it often. Add the green beans and cook them for 4 min.

Step 3

Stir in the tomato with water, salt and pepper. Lower the heat and let them cook for 10 min until the veggies are done. Serve it warm.

Step 4

Get a large mixing bowl:

Step 5

Allow it to cool down completely then serve it with your favorite toppings.

Step 6

Enjoy.

CREAMY JELL-O AND EGG SALAD

Prep Time: 10 mins- **Total Time:** 1 hr 10 mins

SERVINGS : 16

NUTRITIONAL VALUE

Calories 97.9 , Fat 6.8g , Cholesterol 55.9mg , Sodium 104.7mg , Carbohydrates 6.7g , Protein 2.8g

INGREDIENTS

- 8 oz. cream cheese, softened

- 3 tbsp mayonnaise

- 1 C. celery, cut

- 3 oz. lemon Jell-O gelatin

- 1 C. cucumber, cut

- 1 small onion, cut

- 3 eggs, hard-boiled, cut

DIRECTIONS

Step 1

Get a large mixing bowl: Toss in it the celery, cucumber and onion.

Step 2

Get another mixing bowl: Mix in it 1 C. of boiling water with Jell-O. Place it aside to cool down.

Step 3

Get a small mixing bowl: beat in it the mayonnaise with cream cheese until it become smooth. Add it to the veggies with Jell-O and a pinch of salt.

Step 4

Toss them to coat. Place the salad in the fridge and let it sit until ready to serve.

Step 5

Enjoy.

CHICKEN FARM SOUP

Prep Time: 15 mins- **Total Time:** 55 mins

SERVINGS : 16

NUTRITIONAL VALUE

Calories 153.7 , Fat 4.1g , Cholesterol 44.6mg , Sodium 505.8mg , Carbohydrates 14.8g , Protein 15.0g

INGREDIENTS

- 12 C. water
- 3 chicken bouillon cubes
- 2 lbs boneless skinless chicken breasts,
- 2 (14 3/4 oz.) cans cream-style corn
- cubed
- 2 C. uncooked egg noodles
- 1 C. chopped onion
- 1/4 C. butter

- 1 C. chopped celery

- 1 tsp salt

- 1 C. shredded carrot

- 1/4 tsp pepper

DIRECTIONS

Step 1

Place a large pot over medium heat. Stir in it the water, chicken, onion, celery, carrots and bouillon.

Step 2

Cook them until they start boiling. Lower the heat and let them cook for 35 min.

Step 3

Once the time is up, add the corn, noodles and butter to the pot. Let them cook for 12 min.

Step 4

Adjust the seasoning of the soup then serve it hot.

Step 5

Enjoy.

CREAMY CHICKEN ROAST

Prep Time: 20 mins- **Total Time:** 1 hr 50 mins

SERVINGS : 6

NUTRITIONAL VALUE

Calories 368.8 , Fat 32.0g , Cholesterol 117.2mg , Sodium 492.0mg , Carbohydrates 9.7g , Protein 10.8g

INGREDIENTS

- 1 cut-up roasting chicken

- 3 tbsp butter

- 1/2 C. flour

- 1 1/2 C. cream

- 1 tsp salt

- 1 dash pepper

DIRECTIONS

Step 1

Before you do anything, preheat the oven to 350 F.

Step 2

Get a large mixing bowl: Stir in it the flour, salt, and pepper.

Step 3

Place a large pan over medium heat. Heat the butter in it until it melts.

Step 4

Dust the chicken pieces with the flour mix then cook them in the melted butter until they become golden brown.

Step 5

Drain them and transfer them to a baking pan. Drizzle the cream all over the chicken pieces. Cook them in the oven for 2 h.

Step 6

Serve your creamy chicken roast hot.

Step 7

Enjoy.

APPLESAUCE MUFFINS

Prep Time: 20 mins- **Total Time:** 45 mins

SERVINGS : 1

NUTRITIONAL VALUE

Calories 150.4 , Fat 2.0g , Cholesterol 5.0mg , Sodium 77.8mg , Carbohydrates 31.7g , Protein 1.6g

INGREDIENTS

- 1 1/2 C. boiling water

- 1 C. brown sugar, packed

- 1 tsp baking soda

- 1/4 C. butter

- 1 C. dark molasses

- 1/4 C. unsweetened applesauce

- 3 C. flour

DIRECTIONS

Step 1

Before you do anything, preheat the oven to 350 F. line up a muffin pan with Cake liners.

Step 2

Get a large mixing bowl: Stir in the boiling water with soda. Stir in the molasses and place it aside.

Step 3

Get a mixing bowl: Mix in in it the flour, brown sugar and margarine until you get a crumbly mix. Place 1 C. of it aside.

Step 4

Add the applesauce the rest of the crumble mix and combine them well. Pour the batter into the muffin C.. Top it with the remaining 1 C. of crumbs.

Step 5

Place the pan in the oven and let it cook for 22 to 26 min.

Step 6

Enjoy.

VANILLA COFFEE CAKE

Prep Time: 10 mins- **Total Time:** 40 mins

SERVINGS : 6

NUTRITIONAL VALUE

Calories 671.0 , Fat 26.8g , Cholesterol 35.2mg , Sodium 251.7mg , Carbohydrates 103.4g , Protein 5.4g

INGREDIENTS

- 2 C. light brown sugar

- 2 tsp vanilla extract

- 2 C. all-purpose flour

- 1 C. hot strong coffee

- 3/4 C. shortening

- 1 tsp baking soda

- 1 egg

DIRECTIONS

Step 1

Before you do anything, preheat the oven to 325 F. Grease a cake pan and place it aside.

Step 2

Get a large mixing bowl: Combine it the sugar, flour and shortening until they become crumbly.

Step 3

Stir the baking soda into the coffee. Pour it into the flour bowl and mix them well.

Step 4

Mix in the egg and vanilla. Pour the batter into the greased pan. Place it in the oven and let it cook for 32 min.

Step 5

Allow the cake to cool down completely then serve it with your favorite toppings.

Step 6

Enjoy.

BANANA CAKE WITH VANILLA FROSTING

Prep Time: 30 mins- **Total Time:** 1 hr 30 mins

SERVINGS : 12

NUTRITIONAL VALUE

Calories 700.7 , Fat 28.8g , Cholesterol 78.6mg , Sodium 635.0mg , Carbohydrates 107.8g , Protein 6.4g

INGREDIENTS

- CAKE

- PENUCHE FROSTING

- 2/3 C. vegetable shortening

- 3/4 C. butter

- 1 2/3 C. sugar

- 1 1/2 C. brown sugar

- 3 whole eggs, room temp

- 1/4 C. milk, plus

- 2 1/4 C. all-purpose flour

- 2 tbsp milk

- 1 1/4 tsp baking powder

- 1/2 tsp salt

- 1 1/4 tsp baking soda

- 1 1/2 tsp vanilla extract

- 1 1/4 tsp salt

- 3 C. powdered sugar

- 2/3 C. buttermilk

- 1 1/4 C. bananas, mashed

- 2/3 C. chopped black walnut

DIRECTIONS

Step 1

Before you do anything, preheat the oven to 350 F. Grease a 2 cake pans and place them aside.

Step 2

Get a large mixing bowl: Beat in it the sugar with shortening until they become light. Beat in the eggs gradually.

Step 3

Mix in the sugar with flour, baking powder, baking soda, and salt. Add the buttermilk and combine them well until you get a smooth batter.

Step 4

Gold the banana and walnuts into the batter. Pour it into the cake pans and cook them for 36 to 42 min in the oven.

Step 5

Place a heavy saucepan over medium heat: Combine in it the brown sugar with butter until they melt. Cook them until they start boiling.

Step 6

Lower the heat and let them cook for an extra 2 to 3 min while stirring all the time. Mix in the milk and cook them until they start boiling while stirring all the time.

Step 7

Get a large mixing bowl: Pour in it the hot milk mix with vanilla and a pinch of salt.

- 44

- Banana Cake with Vanilla Frosting

Step 8

Add to them the powdered sugar gradually while beating them until they become smooth and creamy to make the frosting.

Step 9

Allow the cakes to cool down completely Spread the frosting all over them. Place them in the fridge until ready to serve.

Step 10

Enjoy.

VANILLA BLONDIES

Prep Time: 40 mins- **Total Time:** 1 hr 10 mins

SERVINGS : 1

NUTRITIONAL VALUE

Calories 222.4 , Fat 6.5g , Cholesterol 41.6mg , Sodium 251.4mg , Carbohydrates 38.9g , Protein 2.4g

INGREDIENTS

- 1/4 C. butter

- 1 tsp vanilla

- 1 C. brown sugar

- 1/2 tsp salt

- 1 egg

- 1 tsp baking powder

- 1 C. all-purpose flour

DIRECTIONS

Step 1

Before you do anything, preheat the oven to 350 F. Grease a cake pan and place it aside.

Step 2

Place a heavy saucepan over medium heat. Heat in it the butter until it melts. Mix in the sugar and keep stirring them until they melt.

Step 3

Turn off the heat and allow the mix to lose heat completely. Combine in the egg, flour, vanilla, salt, and baking powder. Beat them until they become smooth.

Step 4

Pour the batter into the cake pan. Cook it in the oven for 32 min.

Step 5

Allow it to cool down completely then cut it into squares. Serve your brownies or store them in the fridge.

Step 6

Enjoy.

AMISH MINT TEA

Prep Time: 15 mins- **Total Time:** 45 mins

SERVINGS : 1

NUTRITIONAL VALUE

Calories 309.7 , Fat 0.0g , Cholesterol 0.0mg , Sodium 7.9mg , Carbohydrates 80.0g , Protein 0.0g

INGREDIENTS

- 4 quarts water, boiling

- 4 -6 C. sugar

- 1 quart meadow mint tea, stems & leaves Directions

Step 1

Pour 4 quarts of water in a kettle. Heat them until they start boiling.

Step 2

Stir in 1 quart of tea stems and leaves. Heat them again until they start boiling.

Step 3

Once the time is up, turn the heat off and let the tea sit for 1 h while pressing it every once in a while.

Step 4

Once the time is up, discard the leaves and stems. Use a fine cheesecloth to strain the tea.

Step 5

Pour the tea in a heavy saucepan. Stir into 5 C. of sugar and heat it until it dissolves.

Step 6

Let it cool down completely then freeze it until ready to use.

Step 7

To serve your tea, Stir 1 concentrate box of it with 2 to 3 water concentrate boxes.

Step 8

Enjoy.

CRUNCHY BROCCOLI WITH CHEDDAR SAUCE

Prep Time: 10 mins- **Total Time:** 55 mins

SERVINGS : 4

NUTRITIONAL VALUE

Calories 252.9 , Fat 14.0g , Cholesterol 46.9mg , Sodium 820.8mg , Carbohydrates 19.4g , Protein 12.7g

INGREDIENTS

- broccoli

- 2 C. milk

- 2 C. chopped onions

- 1/4 lb mild cheddar cheese

- 4 tbsp flour

- 1 tsp salt

DIRECTIONS

Step 1

Before you do anything, preheat the oven to 375 F. Grease a baking pan.

Step 2

Bring a large pot of water and a pinch of salt to a boil. Stir in it the broccoli and let it cook for 8 min.

Step 3

Place a heavy saucepan over medium heat: Melt in it the butter. Add the flour and mix it well.

Step 4

Add the milk gradually while whisking all the time until you get a smooth and thick mix. Stir in the cheese until it melts to make the sauce.

Step 5

Toss half of the broccoli with onion in the baking pan. Drizzle over it half of the cheese sauce.

Step 6

Top it with the remaining half of the broccoli then drizzle the cheese sauce over it. Place the pan in the oven and let it cook for 48 min.

Step 7

Serve your broccoli casserole warm.

Step 8

Enjoy.

CONDENSED MAPLE TART

Prep Time: 2 mins- **Total Time:** 22 mins

SERVINGS : 1

NUTRITIONAL VALUE

Calories 2826.6 , Fat 96.9g , Cholesterol 143.6mg , Sodium 1646.0mg , Carbohydrates 455.9g , Protein 44.4g

INGREDIENTS

- 1 (14 oz.) cans condensed milk

- 9 inches baked pie shells

- 2/3 C. real maple syrup

- whipped cream

- 1 pinch salt

DIRECTIONS

Step 1

Place a heavy saucepan over low heat. Stir in it the maple syrup, condensed milk and the pinch of salt.

Step 2

Cook them until bubbles starts forming while stirring all the time to make the filling. Turn off the heat and let it lose heat for a while.

Step 3

Pour the filling into the pie shell. Place it in the fridge and let it sit for 3 h in the fridge.

Step 4

Once the time is up, garnish it with some whipped cream then serve it.

Step 5

Enjoy.

SALISBURY STEAK WITH MUSHROOM SAUCE

Prep Time: 8 hrs- **Total Time:** 9 hrs

SERVINGS : 4

NUTRITIONAL VALUE

Calories 433.6 , Fat 21.4g , Cholesterol 85.6mg , Sodium 1045.7mg , Carbohydrates 31.7g , Protein 26.6g

INGREDIENTS

- 1 lb ground beef

- 1 small onion, chopped

- 1 C. milk

- 1 can mushroom soup

- 1 C. cracker crumb

- 1 C. water

- 1/4 tsp pepper

- 1 tsp salt

DIRECTIONS

Step 1

Get a large mixing bowl: Combine in it the beef with cracker crumb, onion, salt and pepper well. Shape the mix into a slightly flat meatloaf.

Step 2

Wrap it in a piece of plastic wrap and place it in the fridge for an overnight.

Step 3

Before you do anything, preheat the oven to 325 F. Grease a casserole dish.

Step 4

Once the time is up, slice meatloaf into thin pieces.

Step 5

Place a skillet over medium heat. Heat a splash of oil in it. Cook in it the meatloaf slices for 4 min until they become golden.

Step 6

Drain the beef slices and transfer them to the casserole dish. Stir into them the mushroom soup with milk and water.

Step 7

Place the casserole in the oven and let it cook for 1 h. Serve it hot.

Step 8

Enjoy.

QUICK CORN AND EGG SOUP

Prep Time: 5 mins- **Total Time:** 20 mins

SERVINGS : 4

NUTRITIONAL VALUE

Calories 407.7 , Fat 5.5g , Cholesterol 46.5mg , Sodium 1430.7mg , Carbohydrates 71.8g , Protein 19.1g

INGREDIENTS

- 2 C. flour

- 1 1/2-2 quarts chicken broth

- 1/2 tsp salt

- 1 (15 1/4 oz.) cans corn, drained and crushed 1 egg, beaten

DIRECTIONS

Step 1

Get a large mixing bowl: Mix in it the flour, salt and beaten egg until they become crumbly.

Step 2

Place a large saucepan over medium heat. Pour in it the broth and heat it through.

Step 3

Stir in the corn and cook them until they start simmering. Mix in the flour mix.

Step 4

Let them soup cook for 12 min while stirring from time to time.

Step 5

Adjust the seasoning of the soup then serve it hot.

Step 6

Enjoy.

SWEET SPICY RAISINS SAUCE

Prep Time:5 mins- **Total Time:** 20 mins

SERVINGS : 4

NUTRITIONAL VALUE

Calories 401.8 , Fat 3.1g , Cholesterol 7.6mg , Sodium 156.1mg , Carbohydrates 98.0g , Protein 1.7g

INGREDIENTS

- 2 C. water

- THICKENING MIXTURE

- 1 C. sugar

- 1 C. water

- 1 tbsp vinegar

- 1/8 C. cornstarch

- 1 tbsp unsalted butter

- 1 1/2 C. raisins

- 1/4 tsp salt

- 1 tbsp cinnamon

DIRECTIONS

Step 1

Place a heavy saucepan over medium heat. Stir in it the sugar with vinegar, 2 C. of water, butter, raisins, salt and cinnamon.

Step 2

Cook them until they start boiling. Lower the heat.

Step 3

Get a small mixing bowl: Whisk in it the cornstarch with water. Stir them into the raisins mix. Let them cook until they sauce become slightly thick.

Step 4

Serve your sauce hot with roast chicken, turkey, meatloaf

Step 5

Enjoy.

RHUBARB ROLLS WITH VANILLA SAUCE

Prep Time: 20 mins- **Total Time:** 55 mins

SERVINGS : 1

NUTRITIONAL VALUE

Calories 438.0 , Fat 11.4g , Cholesterol 20.3mg , Sodium 352.5mg , Carbohydrates 80.8g , Protein 4.4g

INGREDIENTS

- SAUCE
- 2 tsp baking powder
- 1 1/2 C. sugar
- 1/4 tsp salt
- 1 tbsp flour
- 2 1/2 tbsp cold butter
- 1/2 tsp cinnamon
- 3/4 C. milk

- 1/4 tsp salt

- FILLING

- 1 1/2 C. water

- 2 tbsp butter, softened

- 1/3 C. margarine

- 2 C. chopped rhubarb

- 1 tsp vanilla extract

- 1/2 tsp cinnamon

- red food coloring

- 1/2 C. sugar

- DOUGH

- 2 C. flour

- 2 tbsp sugar

DIRECTIONS

Step 1

To make the sauce:

Step 2

Before you do anything, preheat the oven to 350 F. Grease a cake pan and place it aside.

Step 3

Place a heavy saucepan over medium heat. Stir in it the sugar, flour, cinnamon, salt, butter and water. Cook them until they start boiling. let them cook for an extra 2 min.

Step 4

Turn off the heat then stir in the vanilla with food coloring. Place it aside to cool down.

Step 5

To make the dough:

Step 6

Get a large mixing bowl: Mix in it the sugar, flour, baking powder, butter and salt until they become crumbly.

Step 7

Mix in the milk until you get a dough. Place it on a floured surface and roll it until it is 13x

Step 9

Step 8

Get a small mixing bowl: Stir in it the cinnamon and sugar.

Step 9

Place the softened butter over the whole dough. Lay over it the rhubarb and top it with Rhubarb Rolls with Vanilla Sauce

Step 10

Roll the dough over the filling then cut it into 12 rolls. Place the rolls with the open sides facing up in the cake pan.

Step 11

Pour the vanilla sauce all over them. Place the pan in the oven and let them cook for 36 to 42 min.

Step 12

Serve your rhubarb rolls warm.

Step 13

Enjoy.

CARAMEN PECAN CAKE

Prep Time: 10 mins- **Total Time:** 40 mins

SERVINGS : 8

NUTRITIONAL VALUE

Calories 722.6 , Fat 42.8g , Cholesterol 130.0mg , Sodium 731.2mg , Carbohydrates 84.9g , Protein 3.9g

INGREDIENTS

- CAKE

- CARAMEL SAUCE

- 1/2 C. pecans, chopped

- 3/4 C. butter

- 2 1/2 C. cooking apples, chopped

- 1 1/2 C. brown sugar

- 1/2 C. butter, softened

- 3/4 tsp salt

- 1 C. granulated sugar

- 1 1/2 tsp vanilla

- 1 egg

- 3/4 C. heavy cream

- 1 tsp baking soda

- 1/4 tsp salt

- 1 tsp ground cinnamon

- 1 tsp grated nutmeg

- 1 C. flour

DIRECTIONS

Step 1

Before you do anything, preheat the oven to 350 F. Grease a cake pan and place it aside.

Step 2

Get a large mixing bowl: Beat in it the butter with sugar until they become light. Beat in it the egg until they become smooth followed by the baking soda, salt, cinnamon, and nutmeg.

Step 3

Add the flour and mix them well. Fold the nuts with apples into the batter.

Step 4

Pour the batter into the pan. Place it in the oven and let it cook for 32 min.

Step 5

In the meantime, place a heavy saucepan over medium heat. Stir in it the butter, brown sugar, and salt until they melt.

Step 6

Cook them until they start boiling while stirring all the time. Turn off the heat then stir in it the vanilla and the cream to make the caramel sauce.

Step 7

Allow it to cool down completely then serve it with the hot sauce.

Step 8

Enjoy.

STARTE AMISH BISCUITS

Prep Time:30 mins- **Total Time:** 2 hrs

SERVINGS : 24

NUTRITIONAL VALUE

Calories 62.3 , Fat 4.6g , Cholesterol 22.7mg , Sodium 124.4mg , Carbohydrates 4.1g , Protein 1.0g

INGREDIENTS

- 1 C. all-purpose flour

- 1 C. Amish starter

- 1/2 tsp baking soda

- 1/4 C. vegetable oil

- 1/2 tsp salt

- 1/4 C. butter, melted

- 2 tsp baking powder

- 2 eggs, beaten

DIRECTIONS

Step 1

Before you do anything, preheat the oven to 350 F. Grease a baking sheet.

Step 2

Get a large mixing bowl: Stir in it the flour, baking soda, salt and baking powder.

Step 3

Get a mixing bowl: Beat in it the eggs, Amish Starter and oil until they become smooth.

Step 4

Add to them the flour mix and combine them well until you get dough.

Step 5

Flatten the dough with a rolling pin on a floured surface until it becomes 1/2 inch thick.

Step 6

Use a 3 inches cookie cutter to cut the dough into circles. Place the dough circles on the baking sheet.

Step 7

Coat the dough circles with melted butter. Lay over them a kitchen towel and let them sit for 35 min.

Step 8

Place the biscuits in the oven and cook them for 16 to 22 min.

Step 9

Allow it to cool down completely then serve them.

Step 10

Enjoy.

ENDIVE SALAD WITH BACON DRESSING

Prep Time: 15 mins- **Total Time:** 25 mins

SERVINGS : 6

NUTRITIONAL VALUE

Calories 243.0 , Fat 10.8g , Cholesterol 151.5mg , Sodium 616.4mg , Carbohydrates 28.0g , Protein 9.5g

INGREDIENTS

- SALAD

- 2 tbsp flour

- 1 quart endive

- 1 egg, beaten

- 3 hard-boiled eggs

- 1 tsp salt

- HOT BACON DRESSING

- 1/2 C. vinegar

- 4 slices turkey bacon

- 1 1/2 C. water

- 1/2 C. sugar

DIRECTIONS

Step 1

Get a serving bowl: Lay in it the endive pieces. Lay over them the slices eggs.

Step 2

Place a saucepan over medium heat: Cook in it the bacon until it become crisp. Drain it and place it aside.

Step 3

Stir the flour with sugar into the saucepan and mix them well. Mix in it the egg, salt, vinegar and water until they become thick and creamy.

Step 4

Crumble the bacon and stir it into the dressing. Drizzle it over the eggs salad then serve it right away.

Step 5

Enjoy.

HOMEMADE KETCHUP

Prep Time:10 mins- **Total Time:** 3 hrs 10 mins

SERVINGS : 1

NUTRITIONAL VALUE

Calories 352.9 , Fat 0.9g , Cholesterol 0.0mg , Sodium 558.8mg , Carbohydrates 86.2g , Protein 1.5g

INGREDIENTS

- 3 quarts tomato juice

- 3 drops clove oil

- 1 pint apple cider vinegar

- 5 drops cinnamon oil

- 4 -5 C. sugar

- 4 tbsp ground dry mustard

- 1 tsp salt

- 1/4 tsp pepper

DIRECTIONS

Step 1

Place a large saucepan over medium heat. Combine in it all the ingredients. Let them cook for 2 h 35 min.

Step 2

Allow it to cool down completely. Pour the mix into mason jars. Place them in them in the fridge until ready to serve.

Step 3

Enjoy.

CLASSIC CHEESE CORN

Prep Time: 10 mins- **Total Time:** 12 mins

SERVINGS : 1

NUTRITIONAL VALUE

Calories 527.6 , Fat 25.6g , Cholesterol 69.8mg , Sodium 352.8mg , Carbohydrates 62.2g , Protein 22.4g

INGREDIENTS

- 2 ears corn

- 1 pinch cayenne pepper

- 1/2 C. Swiss cheese, diced

- 1 pinch salt

- 2 tsp butter, very soft

DIRECTIONS

Step 1

Bring a large pot of water to a boil. Place in it the corn cobs and let them cook for 3 min.

Step 2

Once the time is up, drain them and pat them dry with some paper towels. Scrap the kernels from the cobs into a mixing bowl with a sharp knife.

Step 3

Stir in the butter with cheese and cayenne pepper into the corn kernels while they are hot.

Step 4

Adjust the seasoning of your salad then serve it right away.

Step 5

Enjoy.

PEANUT CRACKERS

Prep Time:25 mins- **Total Time:** 1 hr 25 mins

SERVINGS : 15

NUTRITIONAL VALUE

Calories 257.9 , Fat 12.6g , Cholesterol 8.1mg , Sodium 50.0mg , Carbohydrates 34.2g , Protein 5.0g

INGREDIENTS

- 1 C. brown sugar

- 4 tbsp butter

- 1 C. light molasses

- 2 C. shelled peanuts

- 1 C. water

- 1 dash salt

DIRECTIONS

Step 1

Line up and grease baking sheet.

Step 2

Place a saucepan over low heat: Stir in it the sugar, molasses, water and salt.

Step 3

Let them cook until they reach a temperature of 280 F.

Step 4

Mix in the butter until it melts. Turn off the heat and fold the peanuts into the mix.

Step 5

Pour the mix in the baking sheet. Place it aside until it cools down completely cools down and harden.

Step 6

Break it into pieces.

Step 7

Enjoy.

SWEET AND SALTY BEEF CHILI

Prep Time: 30 mins- **Total Time:** 1 hr

SERVINGS : 6

NUTRITIONAL VALUE

Calories 326.5 , Fat 12.3g , Cholesterol 51.4mg , Sodium 874.5mg , Carbohydrates 35.1g , Protein 20.3g

INGREDIENTS

- 1 lb ground beef
- 4 C. tomato juice
- 1/2 C. chopped onion
- 2 -3 tbsp chili powder
- 1/2 C. chopped celery
- 16 oz. kidney beans
- 3 tbsp flour
- salt and pepper
- 1/4 C. brown sugar
- 1/4 C. ketchup

DIRECTIONS

Step 1

Place a large pot over medium heat. Cook in it the beef, onions and celery for 8 min. Discard the excess fat.

Step 2

Mix in the flour and cook them for 2 min. Stir in the sugar with ketchup, tomato juice, chili powder, beans, a pinch of salt and pepper.

Step 3

Put on the lid and let the stew cook for 32 min. Serve it hot.

Step 4

Enjoy.

SUNNYCORNBREAD

Prep Time: 10 mins- **Total Time:** 30 mins

SERVINGS : 4

NUTRITIONAL VALUE

Calories 473.1 , Fat 20.8g , Cholesterol 61.4mg , Sodium 767.0mg , Carbohydrates 63.5g , Protein 9.2g

INGREDIENTS

- 1 C. sifted flour

- 1 egg, well beaten

- 1/4 C. sugar

- 1 C. milk

- 1 tbsp baking powder

- 5 tbsp shortening, melted and cooled

- 3/4 tsp salt

- 1 C. yellow cornmeal

DIRECTIONS

Step 1

Before you do anything, preheat the oven to 425 F. Grease a loaf pan and place it aside.

Step 2

Get a large mixing bowl: Stir in it the flour with sugar, baking powder, salt and cornmeal.

Step 3

Get another mixing bowl: Whisk in it the milk with egg and shortening.

Step 4

Mix in the flour mix until they become smooth. Pour the batter into the loaf pan and cook it in the oven for 22 min.

Step 5

Allow the cornbread to sit for 5 min in the pan then place it aside to lose heat completely and serve it.

Step 6

Enjoy.

GLAZED CRISCO PUFFS

Prep Time: 30 mins- **Total Time:** 35 mins

SERVINGS : 1

NUTRITIONAL VALUE

Calories 431.1 , Fat 15.7g , Cholesterol 0.3mg , Sodium 60.9mg , Carbohydrates 70.7g , Protein 2.6g

INGREDIENTS

- 9 C. cake flour

- 1/4 C. cornstarch

- 1 tsp salt

- 3 tbsp evaporated milk

- 3 C. Crisco shortening

- 1/2 tsp vanilla

- 2 tbsp sugar

- 1 1/4 C. water

- 2 C. water

- GLAZE

- 4 lbs powdered sugar

DIRECTIONS

Step 1

Get a large mixing bowl: Combine in it the cake flour with salt, sugar and water until you get a dough.

Step 2

Roll the dough on a lightly floured surface. Cut it into circles of the size you desire. Place a 1 tbsp of the filling you want on the side of each circle.

Step 3

Pull the dough over the filling and press the edges to seal them.

Step 4

Place a deep pan over medium heat. Melt in it the shortening. Cook in it the puffs until they become golden brown.

Step 5

Drain them and place them aside.

Step 6

Get a mixing bowl: Mix in it the powdered sugar with cornstarch, milk, vanilla and water to make the glaze.

Step 7

Drizzle the glaze over the puffs then serve them.

Step 8

Enjoy.

VALENTINE STRAWBERRY AMISH BREAD

Prep Time: 15 mins- **Total Time:** 1 hr

SERVINGS : 10

NUTRITIONAL VALUE

Calories 239.7 , Fat 12.8g , Cholesterol 63.9mg , Sodium 287.4mg , Carbohydrates 26.8g , Protein 5.3g

INGREDIENTS

- 1 1/2 C. Amish starter
- 1 1/2 tsp baking powder
- 3 eggs
- 1/2 tsp baking soda
- 1/2 C. oil
- 1/2 tsp salt
- 1/2 C. applesauce
- 1 1/2 C. sliced strawberries
- 1/2 C. buttermilk
- 1 tbsp sugar
- 2 (1/3 oz.) box sugar-free strawberry
- gelatin mix
- 1/4 C. sugar
- 2 C. flour

DIRECTIONS

Step 1

Before you do anything, preheat the oven to 325 F. Grease 5 small bread pans and place them aside.

Step 2

Get a large mixing bowl: Whisk in it the Amish starter with eggs, oil, applesauce, and buttermilk well.

Step 3

Get a mixing bowl: Add to it the gelatin mix with sugar, flour, baking powder, baking soda, and salt. Mix them well.

Step 4

Get another mixing bowl: Stir in it the strawberries with 1 tbsp of sugar. Fold it into the batter.

Step 5

Pour the batter into the greased pan. Place them in the oven and let them cook for 48

min.

Step 6

Allow the bread pans to cool down completely then serve them.

Step 7

Enjoy.

SPICY ORANGE BREAD

Prep Time: 20 mins- **Total Time:** 1 hr 10 mins

SERVINGS : 15

NUTRITIONAL VALUE

Calories 179.8 , Fat 8.4g , Cholesterol 42.3mg , Sodium 172.8mg , Carbohydrates 23.2g , Protein 3.1g

INGREDIENTS

- 1 1/2 C. Amish starter

- 1 1/2 tsp baking powder

- 3 eggs

- 1/2 tsp baking soda

- 1/2 C. oil

- 1 1/2 tsp allspice

- 1/2 C. applesauce

- 1/2 tsp cinnamon

- 1/2 C. orange juice

- 1/2 tsp salt

- 1 (1/3 oz.) box sugar-free orange Jell-O

- 1 C. dried cranberries

- mix

- 1 tbsp orange zest

- 1/2 C. sugar

- 1 C. pecans

- 2 C. flour

DIRECTIONS

Step 1

Before you do anything, preheat the oven to 350 F. Grease 5 small bread pans and place them aside.

Step 2

Get a large mixing bowl: Whisk in it the starter with eggs, oil, applesauce, and orange juice.

Step 3

Mix in it the orange Jell-O with flour, sugar, baking powder, baking soda, allspice, cinnamon and salt.

Step 4

Fold into them the cranberries with orange zest and pecans. Pour the batter into the pans. Cook them in the oven for 48 min.

Step 5

Allow them to cool down completely then serve them.

Step 6

Enjoy.

POPPY BREAD

Prep Time: 10 mins- **Total Time:** 3 hrs 40 mins

SERVINGS : 12

NUTRITIONAL VALUE

Calories 160.7 , Fat 3.1g , Cholesterol 0.0mg , Sodium 391.1mg , Carbohydrates 28.7g , Protein 5.2g

INGREDIENTS

- 1 C. hot water
- 1 tbsp wheat flakes
- 1 C. Amish starter
- 1 tbsp whole oat groats
- 1 tbsp oil
- 1 tbsp millet
- 2 tbsp brown sugar
- 1 tbsp flax seed

- 2 tsp salt

- 1 tbsp poppy seed

- 2 C. bread flour

- 1 tbsp sesame seeds

- 1 1/2 C. wheat flour

- 1 tbsp sunflower seeds

- 2 tsp active dry yeast

- MULTIGRAIN MIX

- 1 tbsp rye flakes

DIRECTIONS

Step 1

Combine all the ingredients in a bread machine by following the instructions of the manufacturer.

Step 2

Select the French bread setting and let it cook.

Step 3

Enjoy.

SPLENDA MUFFINS

Prep Time: 40 mins- **Total Time:** 1 hr

SERVINGS : 12

NUTRITIONAL VALUE

Calories 60.4 , Fat 3.1g , Cholesterol 24.8mg , Sodium 130.4mg , Carbohydrates 6.6g , Protein 1.6g

INGREDIENTS

- cooking spray

- 3/4 C. milk

- 3/4 C. yellow cornmeal

- 1/2 C. Amish starter

- 1/4 tsp salt

- 2 tbsp butter, melted

- 1/2 tsp baking soda

- 1 tbsp Splenda artificial sweetener

- 1 egg, beaten

DIRECTIONS

Step 1

Before you do anything, preheat the oven to 375 F. Grease 12 C. muffin tin and place it aside.

Step 2

Get a large mixing bowl: Mix in it the cornmeal, salt, baking soda and Splenda.

Step 3

Get another mixing bowl: Whisk in it the eggs, milk, starter and melted butter. Add to them the cornmeal mix while stirring them all the time.

Step 4

Pour the batter into the greased muffin tin. Place it in the oven and let it cook for 40 to 50

min.

Step 5

Allow them to cool down completely then serve them.

Step 6

Enjoy.

NUTTY CARROT MUFFINS

Prep Time: 10 mins- **Total Time:** 30 mins

SERVINGS : 14

NUTRITIONAL VALUE

Calories 132.2 , Fat 3.7g , Cholesterol 15.4mg , Sodium 276.9mg , Carbohydrates 21.3g , Protein 3.9g

INGREDIENTS

- 3/4 C. Amish starter
- 1 tbsp brown sugar
- 1 egg, beaten
- 1 1/2 C. flour
- 1/2 C. buttermilk
- 1 tsp baking soda
- 1/2 C. pureed sweet potato
- 1/2 C. shredded carrot
- 1 tsp vanilla
- 1/2 C. raisins
- 1/2 C. fiber cereal
- 1/2 C. chopped walnuts
- 1/2 C. oats
- 1 tsp salt
- 2 tbsp Splenda artificial sweetener

DIRECTIONS

Step 1

Before you do anything, preheat the oven to 375 F. Grease 12 C. muffin pan and place it aside.

Step 2

Get a large mixing bowl: Cream in it the starter with vanilla, egg, sweet potato, and buttermilk.

Step 3

Mix in the cereal with oats, salt, Splenda, brown sugar, flour, and baking soda. Fold the carrot with raisins and walnuts into the batter.

Step 4

Pour the batter into the muffin pan. Place it in the oven and let it cook for 25 to 30 min.

Step 5

Allow them to cool down completely then serve them.

Step 6

Enjoy.